D1604643

Searchlight
BOOKS™

What
Is a
Food Web?

Desert
Food Webs
in Action

Paul Fleisher

Lerner Publications Company
Minneapolis

Lerner Publications Company
A division of Lerner Publishing Group, Inc.
241 First Avenue North
Minneapolis, MN 55401 U.S.A.

Website address: www.lernerbooks.com

Library of Congress Cataloging-in-Publication Data

Fleisher, Paul.
     Desert food webs in action / by Paul Fleisher.
          p.   cm. — (Searchlight books™—what is a food web?)
     Includes index.
     ISBN 978-1-4677-1294-1 (lib. bdg. : alk. paper)
     ISBN 978-1-4677-1773-1 (eBook)
     1. Desert ecology—Juvenile literature. 2. Desert plants—Juvenile literature.
     3.Desert animals—Juvenile literature. I. Title.
     QH541.5.D4F54 2014
     577.54—dc23   2012032545

Manufactured in the United States of America
1 – BP – 7/15/13

Contents

A DESERT FOOD WEB

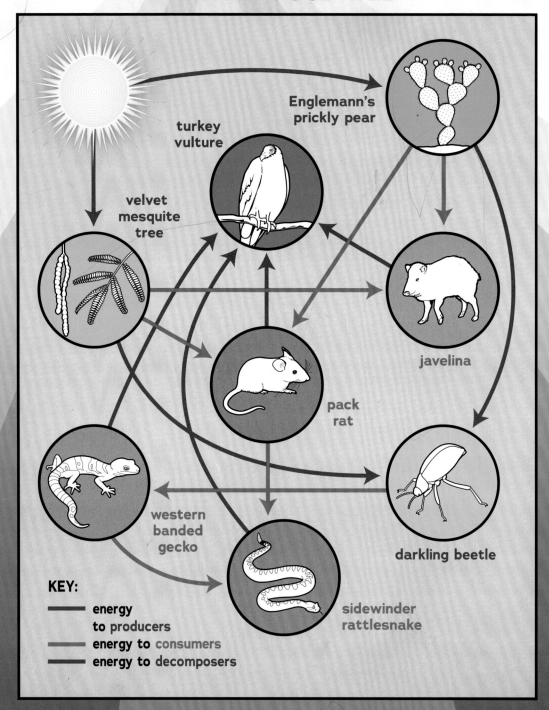

turkey vulture

Englemann's prickly pear

velvet mesquite tree

javelina

pack rat

western banded gecko

sidewinder rattlesnake

darkling beetle

KEY:
— energy to producers
— energy to consumers
— energy to decomposers

Chapter 1

DESERTS

Desert lands are very dry. The ground is rocky and dusty. Some deserts are flat. Other deserts have hills or mountains.

Deserts do not get much rain. Some years, no rain falls. Desert creatures must live with very little water.

This desert in Arizona is sandy and dry. Tall rocks jut out of the ground. What are other deserts like?

A rattlesnake
hides in some
cactuses.

Desert Plants and Animals

Even though the desert is dry, many plants and animals
live there. Cactuses thrive in the desert. Some small
trees live there too. Grasses and flowers also sprout in
the desert.

Snakes and lizards live in the desert. So do rabbits.
Mice scurry among the stones. Many different birds
make nests in the desert. Deer and mountain lions also
live there.

The desert is an important environment. An environment is the place where any creature lives. The environment includes the air, soil, and weather. It also includes other plants and animals.

EARTH'S DESERTS

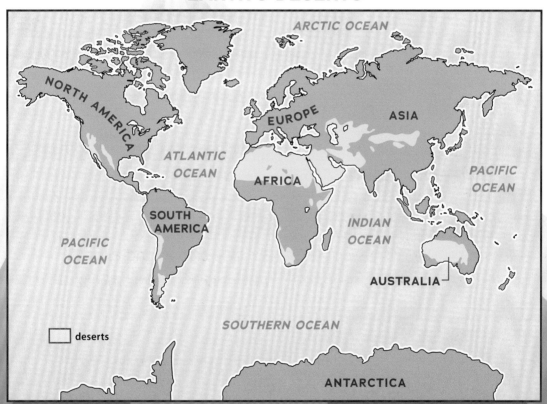

About one-eighth of the world's land is desert. The largest desert is the Sahara. It is in northern Africa.

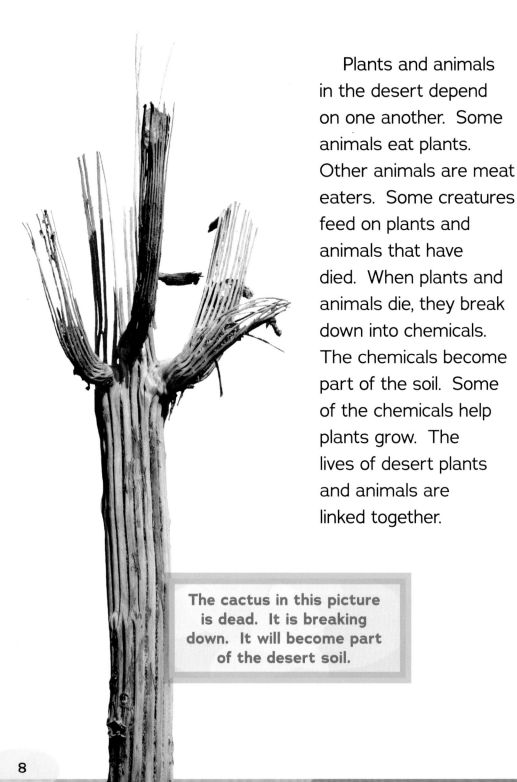

Plants and animals in the desert depend on one another. Some animals eat plants. Other animals are meat eaters. Some creatures feed on plants and animals that have died. When plants and animals die, they break down into chemicals. The chemicals become part of the soil. Some of the chemicals help plants grow. The lives of desert plants and animals are linked together.

The cactus in this picture is dead. It is breaking down. It will become part of the desert soil.

Food Chains

Energy moves from one living thing to another. Living things get energy from food. A food chain shows how the energy moves. Each food chain begins with sunlight. Plants store the sun's energy. They store it as food in their roots and leaves. Animals eat the plants. They get some of the sun's energy from the plants. When one creature eats another, the energy moves along the food chain.

A bee crawls on a cactus flower. It drinks juice from the flower. The bee gets some of the cactus's energy from the juice.

A desert has many food chains. Here is one example. Plants use the sun's energy to make seeds. A rat eats the seeds. Some energy goes from the plant to the rat. Then a hawk eats the rat. Energy passes from the rat to the hawk. When the hawk dies, young flies and beetles eat its body. They get energy from the hawk.

A KANGAROO RAT GETS ENERGY BY EATING PLANT SEEDS. RATS AND MICE ARE FOOD FOR MANY LARGE DESERT ANIMALS.

Food Webs

A food web is made of many food chains. Rats eat many kinds of seeds. They also eat fruit, roots, and even insects. Hawks eat squirrels, snakes, and other small animals. Flies and beetles eat many different dead animals. All the foods the animals eat are part of a food web. A food web shows how all creatures in an environment depend on one another for food.

This hawk is feeding its babies meat from a small animal. Hawks get energy by eating other animals.

Chapter 2

DESERT PLANTS

Green plants use sunlight to make food. Living things that make their own food are called producers. Animals use the food plants produce. Plants also make oxygen. Oxygen is a gas in the air. Animals need oxygen to breathe.

A desert's energy comes from the sun. Desert plants use sunlight to make food. What else do plants make?

Photosynthesis

Plants make food and oxygen through photosynthesis. Plants need sunlight and water for photosynthesis. They also need carbon dioxide. Carbon dioxide is a gas in the air. Plants take in carbon dioxide and sunlight. Their roots take in water.

HOW PHOTOSYNTHESIS WORKS

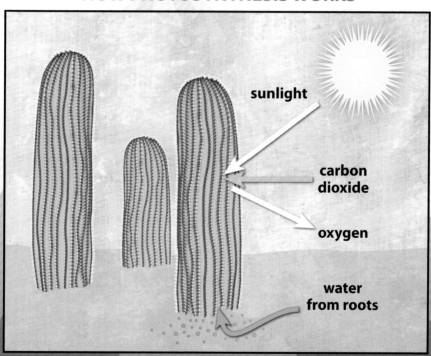

sunlight

carbon dioxide

oxygen

water from roots

The stem of a barrel of cactus turns sunlight, carbon dioxide, and water into food for the cactus.

Using the sun's energy, plants turn water and carbon dioxide into sugar and starch. Sugar and starch are the plants' food. Plants store the food in their leaves, stems, and roots.

As plants make food, they also make oxygen. The oxygen goes into the air. Animals breathe the oxygen. They breathe out carbon dioxide. Plants use the carbon dioxide to make more food.

Plants make oxygen that animals breathe. This desert animal is a chuckwalla.

A paloverde tree shades the ground beneath it. This keeps the soil from drying out in the hot sun.

Nutrients

Plants grow in soil. The soil contains chemicals called nutrients. Living things need nutrients to grow. Water soaks into the soil. Nutrients from the soil go into the water. The plants' roots take in the water and get nutrients from the soil. The nutrients become part of each plant.

Living with Little Water

Plants need water. But the desert has very little water. Desert plants cannot grow close together. There is not enough water to share. So the desert has a lot of bare ground.

Creosote bushes do not share water. Their roots make a special chemical. The chemical keeps other plants away. The creosote bushes get all the water in the soil.

Creosote bushes grow in clumps.

Leaves use lots of water. So desert trees lose their leaves when it gets too dry. Without leaves, they can live with very little water. Paloverde trees have green bark. When they lose their leaves, their bark makes food.

Mesquite trees grow in the desert. Their roots reach deep into the ground to get water. Mesquite trees produce many seeds.

THE SEEDS OF A MESQUITE TREE ARE FOOD FOR MANY DESERT ANIMALS.

Cactuses grow in the desert. Cactuses do not have leaves. They have sharp spines instead. Cactuses make food with their skin. Their thick skin holds in water. That lets them grow even when it is very dry. Cactuses live for many years. A saguaro cactus can be more than one hundred years old.

FLOWERS BLOOM ON A CACTUS. THE FLOWERS ATTRACT BIRDS AND INSECTS. THE CACTUS'S SPINES WARN OTHER HUNGRY ANIMALS TO STAY AWAY.

Desert wildflowers
bloom after a
spring rainfall.

Some desert plants live only a short time. Their seeds
wait in the ground. When it rains, the seeds sprout.
The new plants grow quickly. They bloom. The desert
becomes a beautiful garden. Bees and butterflies visit
the flowers. The flowers make new seeds. Then the
plants die. But the new seeds wait in the soil. They wait
for the next rainfall.

Daisies and poppies sprout after it rains. Sunflowers sprout too. Grasses also grow after a rainfall.

Lichens grow on desert rocks. Lichens are fungi and algae growing together. At night, dew forms on the rocks. Lichens get most of their water from dew.

Colorful lichens grow on rocks. Lichens are plantlike living things.

Chapter 3

DESERT PLANT EATERS

Living things that eat other living things are consumers. *Consume* means "eat." Animals are consumers. Animals that eat plants are called herbivores. The sun's energy is stored in plants. When animals eat plants, they get the sun's energy.

A desert tortoise eats the fruit of a prickly pear cactus. What are animals that eat plants called?

Ants and Caterpillars

Harvester ants are herbivores. They gather seeds to eat. They carry the seeds back to their nest. They store the seeds in the ground. Some of the seeds sprout when it rains. Caterpillars are herbivores too. Caterpillars eat leaves. Later, the caterpillars become butterflies. Butterflies are also herbivores. They drink from desert flowers.

A harvester ant carries a thistle seed.

Birds

Many birds are herbivores. Hummingbirds sip sweet liquid from desert flowers. Quails scratch the soil to dig up seeds. Finches and sparrows eat seeds too.

A quail looks for food in the desert. Quails eat seeds, fruit, or berries that fall to the ground.

Mammals

Mammals can also be herbivores. Pack rats are small mammals that are herbivores. They eat seeds. They store seeds in their burrows. Javelinas look like pigs. They eat the juicy stems of prickly pear cactuses. They eat cactus fruit and seeds from trees. Javelinas also dig for roots.

A javelina uses its long teeth to bite into the pad of a prickly pear cactus. Javelinas are also known as collared peccaries.

Chapter 4

DESERT MEAT EATERS

Some desert creatures eat meat. These animals are called carnivores. They catch and eat other animals. But carnivores also depend on plants. Carnivores get energy by eating animals that have eaten plants.

Meerkats live in Africa. They hunt for other animals to eat. What are animals that eat meat called?

Spiders and Ants

Spiders are carnivores. Some spiders trap insects in their webs. Tarantulas hide in burrows. They catch insects to eat.

Many ants are carnivores. They eat insects and other small animals. Scorpions also hunt small animals for food.

A scorpion can snap up insects, spiders, and centipedes in its large pincers. It can also sting other animals with the tip of its tail.

Birds

Many desert birds eat other animals. Woodpeckers peck cactuses to reach insects living inside. Roadrunners hunt lizards, mice, and snakes. Golden eagles soar high in the sky. They look for small animals. Eagles catch animals in their sharp claws.

Roadrunners are fast runners. This roadrunner was quick enough to grab a small rattlesnake.

Snakes, Lizards, and Mammals

Some deserts get very hot. During the day, many animals hide in the shade. It is cooler at night. Then snakes and lizards come out to hunt. The banded gecko is a lizard. It hunts at night. It hunts insects to eat. Rattlesnakes catch mice and other small mammals.

Mountain lions are mammals that are carnivores. They eat everything from deer to squirrels.

A rattlesnake swallows a small mammal.

Omnivores

Some desert animals eat both plants and animals. These animals are called omnivores. Omnivores eat many different things. Coyotes are omnivores. They hunt small mammals and lizards. Coyotes also eat birds and eggs. They even eat fruit.

A COYOTE SEARCHES FOR DESERT PLANTS AND ANIMALS TO EAT. COYOTES EAT WHATEVER THEY CAN FIND.

Chapter 5

DESERT DECOMPOSERS

When plants and animals in the desert die, they decay. They break down into nutrients. Living things called decomposers help dead things decay. Decomposers feed on dead plants and animals.

This is a dead cactus. It is slowly breaking down. What helps it break down?

Decomposers are nature's recyclers. They help break down dead plants and animals. Nutrients in the dead plants and animals go back into the soil. Then other living things can use the nutrients. Without decomposers, the desert would be full of dead things. Then no new plants could grow. Animals would run out of food.

A dead camel decays in a desert in Asia. Tiny decomposers turn its body into nutrients. Plants use the nutrients to grow.

Ants and Other Insects

Many insects feed on dead things. Ants often eat dead animals. Some insects eat dead plants. When a cactus dies, insects feed on it. The soft parts of the cactus decay. After a while, just a few bits of wood are left. When a tree dies, termites eat the wood. They slowly turn the wood into soil.

Darkling beetles eat dead plants. They also eat dead insects.

Birds

Birds can help break down dead things. Vultures fly over the desert. They search for dead animals to eat.

A TURKEY VULTURE STANDS ON A DEAD ANIMAL. VULTURES CAN SEE AND SMELL DEAD ANIMALS FROM VERY FAR AWAY.

Fungi and Bacteria

Fungi and bacteria feed on dead plants and animals. Bacteria are much too small to see. But they are very important decomposers.

Bacteria and fungi work slowly in the desert. That is because the desert is dry. Bacteria and fungi grow best when it is damp. So dead things rot very slowly in the desert.

Fungi grow on plants, such as this dead cactus. Bacteria also grow on the cactus.

Chapter 6

PEOPLE AND DESERTS

People live in the desert too. They like the sunshine. They like the clean, dry air. They enjoy seeing desert plants and animals. People build cities in the desert. But big cities use lots of water. And the desert does not have much water.

People build villages, towns, and cities in the desert. What can happen when a desert city gets too big?

A river flows through the desert. Many desert streams and rivers appear only after it rains. Then they dry up again.

Rivers carry water through the desert. People get water from the rivers. People dig deep wells to find water underground. But many people want to live in the desert. The desert does not have enough water for everyone.

Handle with Care

People in the desert must use water carefully. They must save water when they bathe and wash. They should not grow grass lawns. Lawns need too much water. People should grow plants that live in dry soil.

Deserts are beautiful. But we need to take care of them. It's important to treat desert plants and animals with care.

This Harris's hawk perches atop a cactus.

Glossary

bacteria: tiny living things made of just one cell. Bacteria can be seen only under a microscope.

cactus: a desert plant that has thick skin and spines instead of leaves

carnivore: an animal that eats meat

consumer: a living thing that eats other living things

decay: to break down

decomposer: a living thing that feeds on dead plants and animals and breaks them down into nutrients

environment: a place where a creature lives. An environment includes the air, soil, weather, plants, and animals in a place.

food chain: the way energy moves from the sun to a plant, then to a plant eater, then to a meat eater, and finally to a decomposer

food web: many food chains connected together. A food web shows how all living things in a place need one another for food.

herbivore: an animal that eats plants

lichen: a plantlike living thing that is part algae and part fungi

mammal: an animal that feeds its babies milk and has hair on its body

nutrient: a chemical that a living thing needs in order to grow

omnivore: an animal that eats both plants and animals

photosynthesis: the way green plants use energy from sunlight to make their own food from carbon dioxide and water

producer: a living thing that makes its own food

Learn More about Deserts and Food Webs

Books

Gowan, Barbara. *D Is for Desert: A World Deserts Alphabet.* Ann Arbor, MI: Sleeping Bear Press, 2012. Discover the world's deserts from *A* to *Z* in this appealing title.

Wojahn, Rebecca Hogue, and Donald Wojahn. *A Desert Food Chain: A Who-Eats-What Adventure in North America.* Minneapolis: Lerner Publications Company, 2009. What you choose to eat shapes your fate in this fun interactive story about food chains.

Zoehfeld, Kathleen Weidner. *Secrets of the Garden: Food Chains and the Food Web in Our Backyard.* New York: Alfred A. Knopf, 2012. This book takes a fun approach to examining food chains and the food web that exist in one family's backyard garden.

Websites

Biomes of the World: Desert
http://www.mbgnet.net/sets/desert/?b467e680
Emily and Roderick take visitors on a road trip through the desert.

Enchanted Learning: Desert Animal Printouts
http://www.enchantedlearning.com/biomes/desert/desert.shtml
This site includes printouts of desert animals such as camels and coyotes as well as factual information on deserts and a map of the world's deserts.

Kid Outdoors—Desert
http://www.kidcrosswords.com/kidoutdoors/where%20to%20go/desert.htm
Find facts about animals, plants, places, and the history of Earth's deserts.

LERNER

SOURCE

Expand learning beyond the printed book. Download free, complementary educational resources for this book from our website, www.lerneresource.com.

Index

Photo Acknowledgments

The images in this book are used with the permission of: © Zeke Smith/Independent Picture Service, pp. 4, 13; © Laura Westlund/Independent Picture Service, p. 7; © Tom Dowd/Dreamstime.com, p. 5; © iStockphoto/Thinkstock, p. 6; © iStockphoto.com/Jami Garrison, p. 8; © Jacek Radon/Dreamstime.com, p. 9; © Richard R. Hansen/Photo Researchers, Inc., p. 10; © John Cancalosi/Peter Arnold/Getty Images, pp. 11, 27, 33; © Photodisc Royalty Free/Getty Images, pp. 12, 19; © Fuse/Getty Images, p. 14; © Tim Fitzharris/Minden Pictures/CORBIS, p. 15; © age fotostock/SuperStock, pp. 16, 21; © Anke Van Wyk/Dreamstime.com, p. 17; © Anton Foltin/Dreamstime.com, p. 19; © Valeriy Kirsanov/Dreamstime.com, p. 20; © Perennou Nuridsany/Photo Researchers, Inc., p. 22; © Rinus Baak/Dreamstime.com, p. 23; © Gerald C. Kelley/Photo Researchers, Inc., p. 24; © Lightpoet/Deposit Photos, p. 25; © Frank Greenaway/Dorling Kindersley/Getty Images, p. 26; © Carlyn Galati/Visuals Unlimited, Inc., p. 28; © Underw atermaui/Dreamstime.com, p. 29; © Andrew Brown; Ecoscene/CORBIS, p. 30; © Ted Wood/Aurora/Getty Images, p. 31; © Ken Lucas/Visuals Unlimited, Inc., p. 32; © Darrell Gulin/CORBIS, p. 34; © Ew amew a2/Dreamstime.com, p. 35; © Lutherbailey/Dreamstime.com, p. 36; © cecoffman/Dreamstime.com, p. 37.
Front cover: © Minden Pictures/SuperStock.

Main body text set in Adrianna Regular 14/20
Typeface provided by Chank